Alain-Fournier · Poems

Alain-Fournier was the pseudonym of Henri-Alban Fournier, a French author and soldier. He was the author of a single novel, *Le Grand Meaulnes* (1913), which has been twice filmed and is considered a classic of French literature. In 1914 he started work on a second novel, *Colombe Blanchet*, but this remained unfinished when he joined the Army as a lieutenant in August. He died fighting near Vaux-les-Palameix (Meuse) one month later, on 22 September 1914. His body remained unidentified until 1991, when he was interred in the cemetery of Saint-Remy-la-Calonne. Most of his writing was published posthumously: *Miracles* (a volume of poems and essays) in 1924, his correspondence with Jacques Rivière in 1926 and his letters to his family in 1930. His notes and sketches for *Colombe Blanchet* have also been published.

Anthony Howell is the author of a dozen collections of poetry and translations, from *Inside the Castle* (1969) to *Silent Highway* (2014). In 1973 he took part in the International Writing Program at the University of Iowa. His translations include *Statius: Silvae* (with Bill Shepherd) and *Plague Lands* by Fawzi Karim, a Poetry Book Society Recommendation in 2011. He founded The Theatre of Mistakes and is editor of *Grey Suit: Video for Art and Literature*.

Anthony Costello is a writer, editor, teacher and horticulturist. His first poetry collection, *The Mask*, was published in 2014 and a second, *Angles & Visions*, in 2016. He is co-editor of *The High Window Journal* and an associate publisher at The High Window Press. He is currently working on a book about artists and their physicians.

Anita Marsh studied English and French at Southampton University. She worked as a language assistant in Belgium, a translator for BNP Paribas and a senior bookseller in London. She had a lifelong love of the French language and French literature and spent her last year living in France and translating the poems of Alain-Fournier. She died in 2013.

T0168933

Alain-Fournier

Poems

TRANSLATED BY

Anthony Howell
Anita Marsh
Anthony Costello

Fyfield*Books*

CARCANET

First published in Great Britain in 2016 by

Carcanet Press Limited
Alliance House
Cross Street
Manchester M2 7AQ
www.carcanet.co.uk

We welcome your feedback: info@carcanet.co.uk

Introduction © Anthony Costello 2016
English versions © Anthony Howell 2016

The right of Anthony Howell and Anthony Costello
to be identified as the authors of these translations, and
as the book's editors and authors of their respective
editorial material, has been asserted by them in accordance
with the Copyright, Designs and Patents Act of 1988.
All rights reserved.

A CIP catalogue record for this book is available
from the British Library, ISBN 978 1 784103 12 5

The publisher acknowledges financial assistance
from Arts Council England

Set in Monotype Fournier by Anvil
Printed and bound in England by SRP Ltd, Exeter

To the memory of Anita Marsh

What will survive of us is love
PHILIP LARKIN

ACKNOWLEDGEMENTS

Acumen: On the Path which Loses Itself, The Early Mists of
      September, The Remains of Warmth, The Shower
Agenda: Road-Song
Orbis: Round-Dance
The French Literary Review: From Summer to Summer

The French texts are based on those in *Miracles*, Gallimard, 1924,
the Livre de Poche edition of Librairie Arthème Fayard, 1986
and the Livre de Poche edition edited by Jacques Dupont, 2011

The frontispiece is from a pencil portrait of Alain-Fournier
by Lavoro, based on a 1913 photograph

The cover painting, *Woman at the Garden*, 1873, by Pierre-Auguste
Renoir, was chosen by Anthony Costello

CONTENTS

INTRODUCTION by Anthony Costello   9

The Poems in English

On the Nacelle   19
I Think of Those   20
The Griefs of Summer   21
Adolescents   22
The Shower   24
Tale of the Sun and the Road   26
On the Great Grey Road   29
Round Dance   32
From Summer to Summer   34
Road Song   38
The Remains of Warmth   41
The Early Mists of September   43
And Now that It's the Rain   45
On the Path which Loses Itself   48

The Poems in French

Sur la nacelle...   55
Je pense à celles...   56
Tristesses d' été   57
Adolescents   58
L'ondée...   60
Conte du soleil et de la route   62
Sur ce Grand Chemin gris...   65
Ronde   68
À travers les étés...   70

Chant de route   73

Sous ce tiède restant…   76

Premières brumes de septembre…   78

Et maintenant que c'est la pluie…   80

Dans le chemin qui s'enfonce…   83

SOME NOTES ON THE TRANSLATION by Anthony Costello   87

NOT SIMPLY THE MEANING by Anthony Howell   91

INTRODUCTION

À tout seigneur tout honneur

ALAIN-FOURNIER, born Henri-Alban Fournier in La Chapelle-d'Angillon, central France, died on 22 September 1914, one month after the outbreak of the First World War. He died, aged twenty-seven, while fighting in Vaux-Les-Palamaix, near Verdun, on the French-Belgian border. It was only in 1991 that his remains were identified and subsequently interred in the cemetery at Saint-Remy-la-Calonne. Obituary writers referred to him as a 'French author and soldier'. Although as a teenager he attended a naval college in Brest for over a year, undertook his military training in 1908–1909 and died fighting for his country, he is best known as the author of *Le Grand Meaulnes*.

Le Grand Meaulnes is regarded as a classic of French literature; a *rite de passage* for young adults on a par with Salinger's *Catcher in the Rye* or Goethe's *The Sorrows of Young Werther*. The eponymous hero of *Le Grand Meaulnes* is an adventurous everyman (or everyboy) of the male imagination, inhabiting that hinterland between the real and unreal, which gives the novel something of the romance that can be found in Novalis and Keats and classic German fairy tales. This strange novel propelled along by the dream-like notions of children, its mythic country settings, its grand châteaux or lost domains, its secrets and its loves and losses, seems of a bygone age. It is a novel where the pursuit and love of a beautiful, mysterious woman (or girl) is a plot in itself, and the *raison d'être* for Meaulnes. Meaulnes' love-interest is Yvonne de Galais, and it is widely acknowledged that the character of Galais represents Yvonne Marie Elise Toussaint de Quiévrecourt, a woman whom Fournier was in love with and (it is fair to say) obsessed with for most of his brief adult life.

We know from Fournier's correspondence with his brother-in-law, Jacques Rivière (a publisher and editor of Marcel Proust in *La Nouvelle Revue Française*), which was published in 1926, and his letters to his family (published in 1930) that Fournier, walking out of the Grand Palais in Paris one day in 1905, became transfixed by a woman he had seen, following her along the Cours La Reine, then on a *bateau mouche* to her home at Saint-Germain-des-Prés, returning several times in the ensuing weeks and eventually speaking to her. Despite being told that she was betrothed to another man, Fournier returned at the same date a year later to see her, but to no avail. It was during the next few years while he was completing his military service that Fournier wrote the essays and short stories and poems published long after his death, in 1924, under the title *Miracles.*

Although Fournier had a love affair with Jeanne Bruneau (the model for Valentine in *Le Grand Meaulnes*) while working as a literary critic in Paris in 1910, and had an affair with an actress, Simone Casimir-Perrier, near the end of his short life, it is Yvonne de Quiévrecourt who is the inspiration for the mysterious 'woman' who pervades most of the poems in *Miracles*, written (1908–1909) at least five years before Fournier gained acclaim by publishing *Le Grand Meaulnes,* which narrowly missed receiving the Prix Goncourt, in 1913.

The poems are a rich resource for our understanding of Fournier as a man, from his country childhood in La Chapelle d'Angillon in the Cher *département* of central France, through the military years and the literary years. Fournier was a critic for the *Paris-Journal* where he met Gide and Paul Claudel and was, for a time, a French tutor to a young T. S. Eliot.

The poems offer a tantalising glimpse into the Alain-Fournier world view. The poet, switching between first, second and third person narration and varying points of view, is always at a point of reflection, reminiscence, moving fluidly (often in adjacent lines) between the past and present and back again.

Fournier was influenced by the Symbolists but the narrative dream-like element to his poetry gives it a substance richer than symbolism. He was also interested in *vers libre* and the work of Jules Laforgue. The poems in *Miracles* possess the transfixing magic of pictures. In Alan Pryce-Jones's lucidly brilliant introduction to the Frank Davison translation of *Le Grand Meaulnes* in 1957, he writes admiringly about the tonality of Fournier's book as containing something of 'the palette of Matisse' and the 'harmonic structure of Debussy'. Pryce-Jones describes the novel as 'high-lit as in sleep', and it is true that the novel and the poems exist in an ambience of particularly striking light and detail. There is too much narrative in *Miracles* for Fournier to be called an imagist poet, but it is the pictures he paints in his poems that remain fixed in the mind.

* * *

In an ideal world Alain-Fournier's poetry would be read in French while listening to the harmonics of Claude Debussy (both Debussy and Fournier admired Maeterlinck's play about the doomed love of Pelléas and Mélisande). The poems might accompany the impressionist paintings of Pierre-Auguste Renoir. A waking-dream-like atmosphere would follow, sense impressions tinged with an awareness of unrequited love, loss, nostalgia, and an almost Proustian search for 'lost time'.

The factual details of the eighteen-year-old Fournier's meeting with Yvonne de Quiévrecourt have been covered in David Arkell's *A Brief Life* and Robert Gibson's *The End of Youth*, but I would prefer to let him narrate the events of this day.

> *I say to her as I pass very close in a tone of voice I shall never recapture, so close that she hears, so quickly as she moves past, and completely spontaneously, "Vous êtes belle."*[1]

And after following her to her house on the boulevard Paris Saint-Germain...

> *I slowly turn around where I wait for the window — it is now that I shall know, it is the moment, the window does not open... and then,*

---

1. *Towards the Lost Domain: Letters from London*, ed. W.J. Strachan (London 1905), Carcanet, 1986.

*all of a sudden, she is coming out opposite me … I whisper to
myself 'Fate' …*

And following her on successive Sundays,

*Where is she going to alight… I think I can see her hand… she is
getting into the tram and alighting from it to go shopping for her
young ladies dresses and negligées… her brown train with a small
tear… her black shoes so open and feminine…*

And so on, until he is rebuffed politely.[2] Yvonne is betrothed to
another and soon to be leaving Paris. But Fournier continues to
love her throughout his life, often despairingly, often with thoughts
bordering on the suicidal, writing her un-posted letters, even
acquiring detective agency reports about her whereabouts in the
next eight years, and declaring his feelings for her again in 1913
after a meeting is set up by Yvonne's sister (after Fournier had
become well known with the publication of *Le Grand Meaulnes*).
Yvonne de Quiévrecourt is the subject of most of Fournier's
poems, with the exception of 'The Early Mists of September', 'The
Remains of Warmth' and 'Road-Song', written while he was on
military service in 1908–1909.[3]

Fournier is the adolescent in love, but the evocations of love
in his poems are not as juvenile as have been claimed. Fournier's
poems didn't gain acceptance in his lifetime. André Gide rejected
Fournier's poems sent to *L'Hermitage*, saying 'this is not the
moment for prose poems',[4] and Jacques Rivière felt they were
'unironic and sentimental'.

---

2. Yvonne de Quiévrecourt tells him 'what's the good' … 'I leave tomorrow …
I don't belong to Paris' … 'we are young' … 'we have been foolish' … 'you have
behaved very respectfully, I do not bear you any ill will at all' … 'I forgive you'
– *Towards the Lost Domain*, op. cit.

3. Alain-Fournier was on 'night manoeuvres' in 1909, walking through the land-
scape of Cagnes that Renoir was soon to preserve in his landscape paintings.
Renoir and Fournier came from similar social backgrounds, both had love affairs
with seamstresses, Renoir fathering a child (to be named Jeanne) to Lise Tréhot,
while Fournier had a brief love affair with Jeanne Bruneau in Paris.

4. David Arkell, *A Brief Life*, Carcanet, 1986, p. 96.

But these views are open to dispute. Most of these poems were written when Fournier was aged eighteen and nineteen; some were composed while he was staying in London in the summer of 1905. His letters at that time, some running to twenty-two pages, are evidence of a mature prose style and contain intelligent and intellectual subject matter. He was reading widely in English – Dickens, Poe, Shakespeare – reading Dostoevsky and attending Wagner's Ring Cycle. He was going to the theatre, visiting The Tate and The National Gallery and making detailed reports on the paintings he saw there (he liked Turner, the Pre-Raphaelites and Braque, and was profoundly affected by Millais' *Ophelia*). He was teaching French, perfecting his excellent English and translating Virgil.

In the letters written and sent from London in 1905 Fournier countered Rivière's comments by arguing that sentimentality only occurs if poems with sentiment as their *modus operandi* are not successful. Fournier was not only being self-consciously sentimental; he believed, finally, in the pastoral over the symbolic, the past over the contemporary. As for Gide's criticism, the prose in Fournier's poems is rather an internalised 'speech-song' – such as Debussy had his singers adopt for his operatic version of *Pelléas and Mélisande*, and hence they eschew rhetoric and are about the truth of adolescent feeling.

In the way that J. D. Salinger was able to maintain the 'voice' of thirteen-year-old Holden Caulfield throughout *The Catcher in the Rye*, so Fournier gives his narrator a younger teenage persona, albeit a perceptive and intelligent one. Fournier was always looking back, and I think he was already setting his recent experiences with Yvonne de Quiévrecourt in the poetic past, the narrator given a naïve outlook, an innocence and an unworldliness that Fournier's real life disavows. The poems are powerful and effective given this distancing, and free-floating in some ideal place and time. Despite the powerful outpouring of spontaneous feelings and the symbolism attached to certain objects in the poems (the château, the parasol, the path, the garden, etc) they are not Romantic in the German or English sense of the word. The poems owe something to the dreamy sense of fantasy attached to French Symbolism, but perhaps ultimately they are shaped more by impressionism and the phenomenology of Husserl and Merleau-Ponty than by the standard preoccupations of nineteenth-century European poetry.

John Taylor feels that when reading Fournier 'we move on to consciously filtered experiencing of the experiencing, from perceiving to apperceiving.'[5] He senses that Fournier's work reveals 'an ontological separation from the *presence* of the world', while Robert Gibson thinks that Fournier's work is in the tradition of Rousseau's *Emile*, Chateaubriand's *René* and Gide's *Les Faux-monnayeurs* – that is, preoccupied with 'The Cult of Adolescence'.[6]

In this sense the poems prefigure the work of Yves Bonnefoy's *L'Arrière-pays*, and serve as a companion to Fournier's novel *Le Grand Meaulnes*, which had as working titles *Le Nom Pays* and *The End of Youth*. John Fowles thought Fournier pinned down an acute perception of the young, which is an awareness of loss as a function of passing time.'[7]

* * *

Looking at the photographs of Fournier in *A Brief Life* – sitting in a high-backed chair at eighteen months in 1888, in school uniform (and with close-cropped hair) at the Lycée Voltaire in 1900, in thinker pose at La Chapelle in 1905, or with fellow officers at Mirande in 1913, it is hard not to be emotionally overwhelmed by knowing that this talented man would be dead a year later, in the first month of the First World War. A year earlier he had been acclaimed as a highly original novelist. Two years previously he had begun building his reputation as a budding writer and critic, seeing his short stories, monographs and reviews published by *La Nouvelle*

---

5. John Taylor, 'A Little Tour through the Land of Alain-Fournier', *The Michigan Quarterly Review*, vol. XXXIX, no. 3, 2000.
6. Robert Gibson, *The End of Youth: the life and work of Alain-Fournier*, Impress Books, 2007.
7. John Fowles, 'Afterword', *The Wanderer*, Signet, 1971.

Revue Française. With the help of Jacques Rivière (who had been his childhood friend as well as now being his brother-in-law) he was moving in literary and artistic circles – Gide, Claudel, Jammes, Péguy, André Lhote – and he was in love with Simone, a famous actress of her day (and later in life a writer and memoirist); he was a man about the city of Paris. He was also a personal assistant to the politician Casimir-Perrier, and his rise from what was considered peasant stock in the region of Bourges in the Cher *département* of central France was still in progress.

Fournier had always fantasised about a life at sea, attending a naval college in Brest for a year when he was fourteen. He completed his military service in 1909. It is easy to suppose that this talented, intellectual, sensitive and creative man might have been unsuited to front-line fighting. Fournier, however, rose to the position of Lieutenant in the 288th Infantry Regiment. He led a group of men into action near Verdun, none of whom returned. Mystery surrounding his death (missing presumed dead) and the difficulty of locating his remains added to the myth of the man who wrote *Le Grand Meaulnes*. The exact whereabouts of the battle Fournier's troops were engaged in has been described in a variety of books: Verdun, Vaux-lès-Palameix, Epargue, Argonne, First Battle of the Marne, Tranchée de Calonnne, Saint-Remy-la-Calonne and Meuse Heights.

Fournier was as elusive in death as the manor house or château or lost domain was difficult to find once more for Meaulnes. The title of *Le Grand Meaulnes* is notoriously difficult to translate: *The Magnificent Meaulnes, The Big Meaulnes, The Lost Estate, The Lost Domain, The Wanderer, Le Nom Pays, The End of Youth* ... It is as if the place names of Fournier's last battle and the names for the novel, and the mysterious and adventure-like chapters of the book ('The Flight', 'The Strange Fête', 'The Meeting', 'The Outing', 'The Secret') are co-morbidities in one massive fatalistic adventure. Ultimately the dreamy countryside of *Clara d'Ellebeuse*[8] is overrun by the machinery of war, with the hostilities commencing in 1914. In a similar way, the art-for-art's-sake palette of Debussy gives way to the more spiky Ravel of the 'Piano trio in A minor'. War poetry is to shake the lyrical foundations of the literary scene in Europe for the ensuing years. T. S. Eliot's *The Waste Land* will be conceived, and Stravinsky's *The Rite of Spring* – indicative of a new aesthetic – while Mark Gertler's *Merry-Go-Round* will be painted in 1918.

If the poems in *Miracles* are to be appreciated fully, and you have found an old recording of Debussy's *Prélude à l'après-midi d'un faune*, then you may be transported to Fournier's 'land of dreams', to his childhood homes of La Chapelle d'Angillon and Epineuil-Le-Fleuriel, and to the beauty of the Sologne countryside. It is a world that doesn't exist any more, and hasn't for the last hundred years. As Marcel Proust wrote in *À la Recherche du Temps Perdu*: 'The true paradises are the paradises that we have lost'.

ANTHONY COSTELLO

---

8. A novel by the French pastoral poet Francis Jammes, whom Fournier admired.

Je ne suis peut-être pas tout à fait un être réel.

BENJAMIN CONSTANT

(quoted by Jacques Rivière
as applied by Fournier to himself)

ON THE NACELLE

On the nacelle,
A parasol
Of satin.

A stain of red,
A breeze to seize
Your hat in.

Through hot shade
A fleeting glint
Of emerald.

All's fresh out here
And on the breeze
The merest hint
Of coastal trees.

A burning though
At noon,
A running tide,
A lighthouse too –

So Isabelle,
You have no need
Merely to dream
Of being freed.

I THINK OF THOSE

I think of those who remain
Frail and brown in their drawing rooms
    At the grey hour
The lamps already lit ...
Those little dresses and dishevelled silks ...
    Our girls.
I think of later hours,
The slow tollings of departure
Urging steps towards the sea,
And the tears that rise
    To fill those lucid eyes.

THE GRIEFS OF SUMMER

Sunday

The curtains are drawn at desolate junctions . . .
The fresh? They've abandoned their spinning, gone outside
For the freshness and the gaiety of far-off greenery . . .
. . . Somewhere inside, a sobbing piano . . .

*

This morning too, because it's summer now,
One thought to have seen them smiling in white.
Already, this morning, the bells have rung out
Because of course it's Sunday . . .

*

Sunlit despair of these desolate afternoons,
Dust . . . silence . . . glimmer of dead gaiety.
Days of lowered curtains, sad as any winter!
. . . And mournfulness here, and exhaustion, and the notes
Of that piano, somewhere, the sob of the forgotten.

ADOLESCENTS

(To Monsieur M. Maeterlinck)

'And seek quietly
With your bloodied hands for what grates on you in the dark.'

About that hill, made drunk with spring,
Having sensed for far too long the dreaming pines
And watched them darken far from town
We went down ... in the evening ... into spring.

We were twenty then, in our thousands.
Our love-sobs strayed across the town.

*

We had crossed each threshold with its arbour,
And brushed against that dear old soul,
The keeper of the path, the hamlet's lullaby
And reader of the dances in the hearth at eventide.

With villages quietly breathing as
We fell to the gathering of the branches ...

*

The glory of the sunset is soon spent,
And in the valley, there is too much moonlight.
The town has gone out, and we go now, less fleet,
Our soles full of holes from the gravel.

Through weeping woods, unsung by any doves,
We stride towards our death with bleeding feet.

*

Hello there! My heart has lost sight of the troupe.
My heart, it's as cold as the moon alone on the moor.
Who's going to show me my route for the dawn?

Who will come to carry down the linen and the lavender?

Along the roads, the carts tonight were bell-like drops
Of shaken light. They're gone now from the moor,
And no Samaritan comes past, as maybe came before.

*

Hello there! Something towers here:
Its shadow wafts across the moor:
A mystery that's there before the dawn!

And in my heart and with each hand
(I find good roads across this land,
How crisp the tone of bells on this new route!
How crisp the tone, when singing of the dawn!)

— And in my heart and in each hand,
In the dusk before dawn, all over the moor,
More lavender found than ever before.

Thrilling the blood, and in each hand
Your marvellous hair, my Melisande!

THE SHOWER

'*a tuft of flowers that trembles with* tears.'

(A. Samain)

The rain brings the children inside as if routed.
The night is slow and fresh with the silence of roads.
In the garden, drop by drop, my heart pours itself out.

She is *so* discrete and pure, but do I dare
Take the risk of loving her? Lovely, please don't delay!
Just come and open the gate one damp evening in May.

*

Timidly, with fingers you mistrust, which tremble now,
You will push it open a little, delighted
By love and by freshness, but with an iota of fright.

The lilacs are heavy with rain at the gate;
Who knows if these, inclining, full of what to declare,
Will quite be able to stop themselves weeping onto your hair?

*

You'll wander gently down the length of the borders
Picking out flowers to put wherever you may
And make of my shivery feelings, a bouquet;

Be careful, though, when crossing to the spot
Where the weeds, tonight, betray a strange allure,
Where the weeds are maddened, dying of their dreams . . .
What if you were to wet your little feet!

*

The high jinks, they're all done,
The mad weeds fast asleep.

The scents of the paths are fading,
And you can come, my welcome one.

All evening, wisely, you will go down the allée,
Warm with love, with petals and dew in your way.

You'll rest your elbows over the brook of my heart,
Unbind your gatherings, flower by flower,
Innocent jasmine, pansies proud from the bower,

And the whole evening's humid, scented dark
Bursting with springtime, showers and delight,
Will be embellished on this peaceful stretch:
Sprigs and flowers turning as they roll towards the night.

TALE OF THE SUN AND THE ROAD

(To a little girl)

There's a little more shade in the squares
Beneath their chestnut trees,
There's a little more sun beating down now on the road.

In ranks of two, a wedding passes by
On this stifling afternoon — a long bridal procession
In all its country finery, remarked upon by everyone.

Look how lost in the midst of it all are the children,
Their fears and upsets ignored.

I think about the One, and one little boy who resembles me.
A light spring morning, under the aspens,

Mild sky scented with dog roses.
He is alone, although he's been invited,
And at this summer wedding he says to himself,

'What if they place me in line next to *her*,
The lovely one who makes me whimper in my bed?'

(Mothers, do you wonder of an evening,
About the tears, the sadness, the passions of your children?)

'I'll wear my big white hat made of straw,
My arm may be touched by the lace of her sleeve,'
As I dream her dream in my Sunday best.

'What a love-filled summer's day we'll see!
She'll be sweetly leaning, on my arm.

I'll take little steps – I'll hold her parasol
And softly say to her, "Mademoiselle . . ."

But firstly, well, in the evening, perhaps,
If we've walked a long way, if the evening is fresh,
I will dare take her hand, I will hold it so tight.
I will speak the truth until I'm out of breath,

And closely now, without the need to fret,
I will say words so tender
That her eyes will go all wet,
And with none to eavesdrop, she will answer . . .'

Thus it is I dream, as my current glances fall
On a mundane groom together with his bride,
Such as one views on any baking noon,
Poised above the steps of a town hall

Then spilling out to music onto the blinding street,
Trailing several couples *en cortège*,
All in their first-time outfits;

Dream, in the dust of this processional affair,
Where two by two go by, the girls with their noses in the air,
Girls in their white, with lace-embroidered sleeves,
And the boys from the big cities, maladroit,
Gripping gauche bouquets of artificial flowers;

I dream about those small forgotten boys;
Panicked, placed last minute with no one in particular;

Dream about the village boys, those impassioned lads
Jostled at a rhythmic pace in these absurd parades;

– Of others caught up in the rhythmical process, confident
And pulled along, heading for a liveliness
Which loves to make a noise, peal without a purpose.

– Of the very smallest – going up and down the rows,
Who can't find their mummies, and one above all

Who looks just like me, like me. More and more,
Above all else, it's him I see, as the sun heats up for joy;
This boy who has lost to that dusty wind that blows,

His nice new hat, of crisp silk-banded straw,
And I see him on the road, chasing after it,
And lost to the march past of belles with their beaus
Runs after it – despite their jeers – runs after it, blinded
By the sun, and by the dust and by his tears.

ON THE GREAT GREY ROAD

'I am closer to you in the dark'

(*Pelléas et Mélisande*, act IV, scene 3)

On that great grey road
To which we have been led by our two byways
Here we are, both caught by shower and storm and night.
With no shelter in sight.
We'll have to take to the ruts,
Seek from these detours the initial lights
Of some far-off land ...
We'll have to head on, hand in hand,
Travelling the grey months,
Lost among the major roads in front of us,
At night ...

*

We can't read the edges of those roads,
We can't read them because of the night,
Because of the starless night, because of the downpour.

*

And before this, we went on, oh so blindly confident,
Pleased with the way things were going, pleased with our lives,
As if we were two little children
On the village street, beneath a great umbrella.

*

We'll take a chance, the two of us, a shadow at a step,
And never blame each other for the night, in the wood,
For the night on our tracks, the night where things get lost.
And then I'll say, 'Come close to me, closer,'
Frightened of losing you now,
Since you have dared to accept my hand tonight

In the frightening dark, with timid fingers too.
So as not to be scared, you let me lead the way for you.

*

We'll get side-tracked sometimes, you and I,
Sometimes find a puddle soaks our ankles;
Flurries of wind, rain and branches hold us up,
And blind our eyes. And we won't want the rain
To last much longer, even if the rain is, in a sense,
The sole sad friend of those who find themselves
Thinking, wide awake, until the dawn,
Who, in bed, alone, with fevered hands,
Listen to it, soothed. They like the company
Of its faint moan across the sleeping plain,
Its rustling in the garden all night long.

*

We shall travel for such hours, for such hours across the plain
And by the end, by the end, exhausted, out of breath,
With heavy heart, you cannot, no, you cannot take another step.
But then it's me, quite suddenly, who will take the load off you,
Your efforts now supported by my lilting stride
Which will be almost like happiness, only because
Now it simply has to be that I take you in my arms.

And then, and then, it has to be those distant ones,
Those first distant glimmers of a place
My tired eyes have searched for, all night long,
Begin to shine, at peace; all of a sudden
The reassuring lamps of village and farmhouse
Lamps of the evening and distant night-lights brighten,
With the entrance, somewhere, to a tavern, brilliance
Of a hostelry, into which I will bring you, my companion,
Into that tavern over there, where for the rest of the night
I will have your heart against my heart . . .

And there, in those coarse sheets with the smell of the country
About them, where we rest our sorely troubled limbs,
Musing on the tranquil goodness of the land,
And going through the night before, and all those frightful roads
— Your skin will be so soft and warm and scented,
The soft tissue of love, your so belovèd body.
The flesh, in which one sleeps, utterly consoling me, your comfort
Will make of those sheets the linen of churches, delicate,
Divine. Sheets of silk and the golden ones one wraps
Carefully around the holy chalices, meant for the blood of those
'Saddened even unto death,' who take the stage
At some late hour, marked but with a cross
Where, silently they've passed away, leaving just a drop
Of humble blood, which women may collect
— So that this precious blood, dripping from their feet
Into those cold chalices, dripping from their gaunt,
Exhausted faces — so that the blood of these Christs
Will drip with less distress and with less cold.

ROUND DANCE

'We won't go back to the wood,
They've cut down all the laurels'

The evening's soft, the round is wild,
Give me your hands, you playful child,
Come and dance beneath the limes.

Your skirts fly off to distant climes,
The evening's blue, my spirit wild,
So turn again beneath the limes! . . .

*

Let's turn until the chill sets in,
Dancing here with 'the lovely one'.

*

The poppet joins the turning round
The square is brown, the dance is blond,
The doorsteps listen to the sound.

My spirit is that little blond;
Of wanderlust we're not so fond,
Let's stay and dance this local round.

*

Dance until the chill sets in,
Turning here with 'the lovely one'.

*

One more, before we're told to stop.
Yes, before we're all grown up,
Let's dance and then we'll go to sleep.

A last dance under the chestnut trees,
A last dance, turning as we please
Till dying brings us to our knees . . .

*

Till dying brings us to our knees.

FROM SUMMER TO SUMMER

(To a young girl
To a house
To Francis Jammes)

Awaited so
Through summers listless in each yard,
Summers which pour down their ennui in silence
Under the ancient sun of my afternoon
Made ponderous through silence,
By loners, lost in visions of love:
Loving beneath the wisteria, its shade
Gracing the yard of some peaceful house
Hidden beneath branches
Spread across my own distances
And my own infantile summers:
Those who dream of love or weep for childhood.

It is you, it is you who have come to me,
This afternoon which lies
Baking in its avenues,
Come with a white parasol
And with a look of surprise,
Quite solemn as well,
And a little bent over,
As in my childhood
You might be, beneath a white parasol.

And of course you're surprised that,
Without planning to have come
Or intending to be blond,
You have suddenly found yourself
Here in my path,
And as suddenly you have brought

The freshness of your hands,
While bringing in your hair all the summers of the earth.

*

You have come
And even my sunniest dream
Could never dare imagine you so beautiful,
And yet, right here and now,
I recognise you.

Right here and now, up close to you,
And how proud you are, and such a proper damsel,
A little gay old woman on your arm;
And it seems as if you choose to lead,
At a leisurely pace surely, and practically
Beneath your parasol, me to the summer-house,
Yes, and to my childhood's dreamy place.

To some peaceful house with nests in its roofs,
While, within its yard, wisteria shadows the doorstep,
Some lovely building with two
Turrets and maybe a name
Like the titles of those prize-awarded books
We used to enjoy in July.

See, you have come to spend the afternoon with me,
Where? Who knows? In *The Turtle-Dove House*?

*

You are going in, you are entering,
Through all the sparrows' chit-chat on the roof,
Through the shadow bars of the gate that shuts behind us,
Shaking down the petals of a climbing rose:
Light petals, balmy and burning: snow-coloured,
Gold-coloured, flame-coloured, fluttering

35

Down onto flower-beds, borders with green benches,
And down each allée festooned as if for a saint's day.
I'm coming too, we are tracing, together
With your dear old thing, this oh so lovely allée.
It's where, this evening, your dress,
On our return, will gather up softly
Scents that are coloured by your tresses.

And then to be allowed, the two of us,
In the dark of the drawing room,
Such meetings as enable us
To celebrate the ritual of sweet nothings.

Or beside you now, reading near the pigeon loft,
On a garden bench where the chestnut
Wafts its shade, using up the evening
Reading to the coo of those doves who are startled
Merely by the turn of a page.
Let's choose a novel of some noble age,
Or *Clara d'Ellébeuse*,

Stay out there, till supper, until nightfall,
Right up to the time when pail gets drawn from well,
And on cooling paths the play of children can't help but amuse.

*

It was there, to be near to my 'far away' fair
I was going, and you never came,
Though my dream was to dog your steps,
But only my dream ever got to you,
Got to that castle, where sweetly vain,
You were the châtelaine.

It was there that we were going surely,
That Sunday in Paris, along that *lointaine*
Avenue made to comply with our dream?
More silent, ever more lengthy, and empty ever after . . .
And then, on some deserted quay, on a bank of the Seine,
And then after that, even closer to you, in the boat,
To the quiet purr of its motor through the water . . .

ROAD SONG

'... main roads where nothing happens'

Jules Laforgue

One invader, then all of them, sing:

We caught the fever
From your marshes,
Caught the fever and we went away.

We had been warned
That we would discover
Nothing but the sun
In the depths of your forests.

We have been through stories
Of broken stretchers,
Lost horseshoes, wounded horses
And worn-out donkeys in a sweat
Stubbornly refusing to advance.

We have lost all memory of those tales
That one tells at the end of the day.
We have lost all hope of the day ever ending.

And now we have taken their saddles
To make shoes for ourselves.
We have set out again, on foot
Through your broom
Which bloodies the feet,
And our feet bleed blood
Till they dry in your dust
As we march,
And so we cure our wounds

By grinding as we go
The balsams and the balms
From your maquis.

We could have sat and waited
In the shelter of your ditches,
Our bodies steaming and tormented.
We had nothing to say, not a shred of hope,
Nothing to say, and not a thing to drink.
We opted for retreat, a rout
Without an end
To highways and horizons:
Defeated horizons which retreated,
And miles left behind in the dust
To entrap those glimpsed from afar
With their signs indicating
Towns with faraway names,
With names which ring like the stones
Of your roads beneath our heels.

We'll not reach the wonderful cities
Which are no more than names with a ring to them,
Cities dead of the sun.

But we still want to live in the sun of your skies
With all our heads aglow
And ring out the rankings of glory forever,
Sending out sparks from our soles;
Sing with the throats of victory
Songs that will send us out drinking again,
For we have caught the fever
At midday from your harsh parched marshes,
From your dust-choked roads
And from your towns which prove mirages.

Caught the fever from your forests without shade
And your tussocks on the dunes
With their russet look, their savage scent:

These are what gave us the fever.

THE REMAINS OF WARMTH

Under what remains
Of a mild September sun,
Perfumed, bright and gilded like a bee,
My mind returns to that little old woman,
An orchard, her small, hurried steps
Ten years ago today.

And just as in previous years
I long to shake down the pears
In that neglected orchard;
Long to believe her there,
Her handkerchief knotted round her head,
Her face crinkled as she concentrates
On her September task,
There, under the pear trees,
Filling up her apron
Or giving over the whole
Of her old village soul
To hanging out the laundry on the raspberries.

In these last balmy days,
I know that she is a spirit there
In the gardens
Half way up from the coast,
And that she expects me,
Since there are always stories to tell
On the bench:
Ancient tales of her youth
Under the dear old sky of September,
And plenty of pears to gather
In the gardens of her children:

Fruit that smells like her cupboard,
It's been ten years, of honey and amber.

Perhaps, back there,
No one now senses
That all of this is her soul
Palpitating gently.
There's no one but me.
Only I can open the gate
And enter
Without troubling the prayer
Of that hushed enclosure and the wilderness orchard
Which so suits her nature.

No one in the village knows,
No one.
And it's me every year
Who makes this pilgrimage
Before the great wild wind of autumn
Comes howling in to shake the orchards,
Using big mad brutal hands
To break the branches, blow forgotten pears
To smithereens, as one evening,
Ten years ago, and every year after that,
After I had gone away,
It came howling, to blow out the candle
And the spirit of the dear old thing,
One evening, down the valleys, from the sky.

THE EARLY MISTS OF SEPTEMBER

'Believe me, it's over for sure, until next year.'

Jules Laforgue

The early mists of September
Over the ferns and heathers,
On the moors, down the rides, in the firs.

The first fires lit in the villages, blazing
From first light, which crackle and glow
In the dark rooms of taverns, on the farms,
As well as in the cottages at dawn.

Coming from afar along the crisp main roads
In his covered wagon,
The hawker stops to chat, to make a sale
And warm his hands.
Leaving his team to clink and steam
Through the half-open doors.
And I glimpse on the walls, by breaks of light,
Before they open the shutters,
The pictures and the daguerreotypes
That will be seen all winter, ruddily shown
Above each hearth, in the dark, low rooms
Of those cottages, taverns and farms:
Elegant ladies in muffs and furs
Situated in snowscapes.

And I hear, 'not warm, this morning.
Here comes a proper chill.
There must have been a frost last night
In the woods on the hill.'

We've seen such lovely summers!
But don't you think this evening
We should seal the château doors?
It's time to get going, get back,
Enveloped in our overcoats,
Down chestnut-guarded roads
Rapidly shedding as we freeze
In our ass-drawn carts and barouches
Loaded with worries and little despairs,
Our holidays over. It's back to our cares.

AND NOW THAT IT'S THE RAIN

And now that it's the rain, and the big January wind,
And the panes of the conservatory,
In which I'm sort of a refugee,
Making little glassy sounds all day,
And the wind, which blows the smoke back down the chimney,
Wresting the Virginia creeper free
So that it tosses wildly down the tunnelled bower,
I don't know where she is. Oh, where is she?

*

There are footprints full of water on the pathways.
They are printed in the soaked-through sand
Of the garden that was our dream in June ...
And now on her way she has gone.

And the house
Where, all summer long,
Under the leaves of its well-watered avenues,
We just imagined our lives going on and on,
Like one simply beautiful season ...

That house, in my heart,
Is abandoned now. It's chilly too,
With its slate roof pale
In the rain, and the sparrows' nests
All dislodged and rotting, dangling from
The cornices and trailing in the gale.

*

It will soon be night,
And the great drizzling wind
Turns up the umbrellas

And makes the ladies' faces wet
As they come from the village and unlatch the gate.

Mon amie,
My lovely girl,
Who isn't here,
This hour I'm in goes by
And the gate never squeaks,
And it's not that I'm waiting,
Not that I lift any curtain to get
Any glimpse of you coming
Through the wind and the wet.

This hour goes by, my dear,
And it's not really one of 'our' hours . . .
But we would have loved it nevertheless
Like all the others of a whole lifetime
Brought to me simply by your serious hands,
The hands of a lovely woman.

*

You have gone on your way.

And it just keeps drizzling down
In each allée,
Where you feel the damp
Up to your ankles.

It drizzles down on the chestnut trees,
Gloomy and confusing,
Wets the benches where,
This summer, in the shade,
You would have been sitting,
And oh how blond you stayed.

It drizzles down on the house and on its gate
And on the yews of the drive,
Where perhaps for the very last time
I do look out, while musing to myself
In the lowest of voices, perhaps
For the very last time of all times:

'She is far way . . . where is she? That serious brow
Pressed against which window sill?'

                    *

At the fall of night,
The dripping shutters
Battering against the windows here
Will need to be properly shut.
And I'll have to go out to the lawn
To bring in that forgotten croquet set
Which is getting wet.

ON THE PATH WHICH LOSES ITSELF

On the path which loses itself at the farm
To sunlight stained with shade, between two hedges
Where the hens go in and then come out again –
There appeared, at the gate of a field,
Having come through the wheat,
And held up now with a negligent gesture,
That laundered dress with its trailed parasol –
It was you, you were back,
You had come by the hazel-tree track,
Back to the mansion of our abandoned passion.

Oh ceremonious friend, far away from me,
You will not find the Fine-House of last summer:
That other summer, that other love is gone,
And what has come back is the harsh sun
Among bumpkins, and all the hovels of old,
Just as it's always been and as it always will be.

Yet still, you're my serious pal,
My silent, my faithful, my faraway friend,
So don't be afraid to turn up or to follow
Me into the homes of those dignified folk,
Silent and slow: real country people;
Go with me into the yard
Where one hitches up the mare
For you to sit yourself
Down on the leather swing
That's burning hot! Which hangs
By two ropes behind the seat of the cart.

Open your parasol,
There, just like that!

The peasant comes to say, 'Mademoiselle,
You will do better up front.'
Say to him sweetly,
As if you existed, 'I won't.'

And let's stay swinging. Shaken so,
You are quite a sight!

We're stopping. Whoa!
There, where the cart-track has turned,
After the escarpments, twists, bends and descents,
Of that back country, into a street:
It's where the wheelwright has his carriage out
To dry, and where, on the side with the shade,
The women sew by dark windows,
And we've drawn up, in the broadest daylight,
There, in front of a house.

Don't be afraid
To negotiate the bridge above the ditch.
Here's the white gate. Do let me lift up the latch,
And under the trellis, here
In the little yard with its walls of bouquets,
At last, a little awkwardly, as before,
Here are your hands
On the black handle of that stiff old door.

They're not expecting us.
No one's come out, shielding an eye,
To peer at who may have arrived.
The carriage goes on its way,
And here we are, the two of us,
Hardly daring to go in, or to push open the wing
That cuts the rustic door in half,
And show ourselves now to the old folks within.

Don't be afraid, except to have not sufficiently
Madly adored that madly impossible day.

And let's be off again! Off towards the roofs,
Spilt between the trees, under the flowering white
Of a blossoming sky, off towards the horizon
Like fragments of pebbles, mirrors in grass, buckwheat flowers...

My little willowy thing,
They would say, on the land,
That your waist would fit
Into the belt of a
Hand joined to a hand.

My blond, my passion manifest,
That yellow hair!
We all want you to wear the crown.
It's you who should be honoured,
With harvest blooms excited by the sun
And gathered at the height of when
The threshing machines can be heard
Snoring all over the countryside,
Then wheezing and expectorating
Straw dust in each yard.

Oh, my very sweet,
I will lay my head, will lay it on your dress,
In the low cool room where we take our ease
And it will be as if, since break of day,
We have been out, among the ripened wheat,
Out in the wheat the whole mad day!
As if the two of us had heard,
On leaving town, the heavy creaking
Of some lowly door, a worm-eaten shutter being eased.
And when we're beyond that, in the fields,

There are the wheezy combines juddering out the rumble of
    their ilk.
And then it will be as if we had come
At dusk to the humble room
Of some strange farm
Simply to ask for some milk.

Miracles

SUR LA NACELLE...

Sur la nacelle
Une ombrelle
De satin.

La tache est rouge
L'eau ne bouge
Ce matin.

Sous l'ombre chaude
Un reflet rôde
D'émeraude.

Et de prés frais
Et de forêts
On sent à peine
L'haleine.

Pour un midi brûlant d'été,
Un ruisseau clair, une tourelle,
Ne va pas rêver, Isabelle,
De soleil et de liberté.

JE PENSE À CELLES...

Je pense à celles qui seront,
Frêles et brunes au salon
    À l'heure grise
Avant les lampes allumées
Petites robes, soies froissées
    Nos filles.
Je pense aux heures de plus tard
Sonneuses lentes de départ
[...] portant leurs pas vers la mer
[...] dans leurs yeux clairs
    De larmes.

TRISTESSES D' ÉTÉ

Dimanche

Les rideaux sont fermés, aux carrefours déserts...
Fraîches, Elles ont quitté le rouet et la porte
Pour la fraîcheur et la gaieté des lointains verts...
... Quelque part, un piano sanglote...

*

Et ce matin pourtant, parce que c'était l'Été,
on avait cru les voir sourire en robe blanche;
Et pourtant, ce matin, les cloches ont chanté
parce que c'était Dimanche...

*

Désespoirs ensoleillés d'après-midi déserts,
Poussière... silence... et rayons des gaietés mortes,
Jours de rideaux baissés, tristes comme des hivers!..
.. Et, pleureuses venues.. et lasses.., des notes
Qu'un piano,.. quelque part.., d'oubliée, sanglote...

ADOLESCENTS

(À Monsieur M. Maeterlinck.)

«. . . et cherchez doucement
Avec vos mains de sang qui s'écorchent dans l'ombre.»

De la Colline – enivrés de printemps,
d'avoir senti rêver les sapins trop longtemps,
et d'avoir regardé bleuir au loin la Ville,
Nous sommes descendus.. au soir.. et au printemps.

Nous étions vingt, nous étions mille
Et nos sanglots d'amour s'en allaient vers la Ville.

*

Nous avons passé les seuils et leurs treilles,
et nous avons frôlé l'âme petite et vieille
gardienne du chemin, berceuse des hameaux,
et familière, au soir, quand les âtres s'égayent.

Au souffle calme des hameaux,
Nous sommes descendus en cueillant des rameaux.

*

La gloire du couchant s'en est allée,
II a fait trop clair de lune sur la vallée,
La ville s'est éteinte.. et nous allons à pied..
à pieds percés aux graviers blancs de la vallée.

En pleurant le bois muet des ramiers,
Nous marchons vers la Mort dans le sang de nos pieds.

*

Ho!.. Mon cœur a perdu le reste de la bande!..
Mon cœur est froid de lune et tout seul dans la lande!..
Qui donc va m'enseigner la route du Matin?

Qui donc viendrait porteur de toile et de lavande?

Les charrettes, ce soir, en grelots aux chemins,
en fanaux cahotés, sont parties par la lande..
.. Il ne passera plus de bon Samaritain.

*

Ho!.. Voici qu'il y a quelque chose sur la lande,
La douce ombre de la Tour sur toute la lande
de la Tour mystérieuse d'être avant le Matin!..

— et sur mon cœur et sur mes mains..
(J'ai retrouvé les bons chemins..
Oh! les grelots sont clairs sur le nouveau chemin..
Oh! les grelots sont clairs de chanter au matin!)

— et sur mon cœur et sur mes mains,
Crépuscule avant l'aube et sur toute la lande,
sur tout mon sang, bonne lavande,

— et sur mon cœur et sur mes mains,
ta chevelure, ô Mélisande!

L'ONDÉE...

« Une touffe de fleurs où trembleraient des larmes. »

(A. Samain.)

L'ondée a fait rentrer les enfants en déroute,
La nuit vient lente et fraîche au silence des routes,
Et mon cœur au jardin s'épanche goutte à goutte

Si discret, maintenant, et si pur... qu'à l'aimer
On pourrait se risquer — Oh! Belle qui viendrez,
Vous ouvrirez la grille un soir mouillé de mai.

*

Timidement, avec des doigts qui se méfient,
Et qui tremblent... un peu, vous ouvrirez, ravie
D'amour et de fraîcheur et de frayeur... un peu:

Les lilas aux barreaux sont encore lourds de pluie...
Qui sait si les lilas, inclinés, lourds d'aveux,
Vont pas pleurer sur vos cheveux!..

*

Vous irez, doucement, tout le long des bordures,
Chercher des fleurs pour vous les mettre à la ceinture
Mes pensées frissonnantes pour en faire un bouquet;

Gardez-vous bien, surtout, de passer aux sentiers
Où les herbes, ce soir, ont d'étranges allures,
Où les herbes sont folles et meurent de rêver!..
Si vous alliez mouiller vos petits pieds!...

*

Les rondes folles se sont tues.
— Les herbes folles vont dormir.
L'allée embaume à en mourir...
Tu peux venir, ma bienvenue!

Tout le soir, sagement, tu descendras l'allée
Tiède d'amour, de pétales et de rosée.

Tu viendras t'accouder au ruisseau de mon cœur,
Y délier ta cueillette, y délier fleur à fleur
La candeur des jasmins et l'orgueil des pensées.

— Et tout le soir, dans l'ombre humide et parfumée,
Débordant de printemps, de pluie et de bonheur,
Les larges eaux de paix, les eaux fleurdelisées
Rouleront vers la Nuit des branches et des fleurs...

CONTE DU SOLEIL ET DE LA ROUTE

(À une petite fille.)

— Un peu plus d'ombre sous les marronniers des places,
Un peu plus de soleil sur la grand' route lasse...

Des noces passeront, aux «beaux jours» étouffants,
sur la grand' route, au grand soleil, et sur deux rangs.

De très longs cortèges de noces campagnardes
avec de beaux habits dont tout le monde parle

Et de petits enfants, dans la noce, effarés
auront de très petits «gros chagrins» ignorés...

— Je songe à l'Un, petit garçon, qui me ressemble
et, les matins légers de printemps, sous les trembles,

à cause du ciel tiède et des haies d'églantiers,
parce qu'il était seul, qu'on l'avait invité,
se prenait à rêver à la noce d'Été:

«...On me "mettra" peut-être — on l'a dit — avec Elle
qui me fait pleurer dans mon lit, et qui est belle...

(Si vous saviez — les soirs, quelquefois — oh mamans,
les pleurs de tristesse et d'amour de vos enfants!)

«...J'aurai mon grand chapeau de paille neuve et blanche;
sur mon bras la dentelle envolée de sa manche...»
— Et je rêve son rêve aux habits de Dimanche.

«...Oh! le beau temps d'amour et d'Été qu'il fera,
Et qu'elle sera douce et penchée, à mon bras.

J'irai à petits pas. Je tiendrai son ombrelle.
Très doucement, je lui dirai "Mademoiselle"

d'abord — Et puis, le soir, peut-être, j'oserai,
si l'étape est très longue, et si le soir est frais,
serrer si fort son bras, et lui dire si près,
à perdre haleine, et sans chercher, des mots si vrais

qu'elle en aura "ses" yeux mouillés — des mots si tendres
qu'elle me répondra, sans que personne entende...»

— Et je songe, à présent, aux mariées pas jolies
qu'on voit, les matins chauds, descendre des mairies

Sur la route aveuglante, en musique, et traîner
des couples en cortège, aux habits étrennés.

— Et je songe, dans la poussière de leurs traînes
où passent, deux à deux, les fillettes hautaines
les fillettes en blanc, aux manches de dentelles,
Et les garçons venus des grandes Villes — laids,
avec de laids bouquets de fleurs artificielles,

— je songe aux petits gars oubliés, affolés
qu'on n'a mis, «au dernier moment», avec personne

— aux petits gars des bourgs, amoureux bousculés
par le cortège au pas ridicule et rythmé

— aux petits gars qui ne s'en vont avec personne
dans le cortège qui s'en va, fier et traîné
vers l'allégresse sans raison, là-bas, qui sonne.

— Et tout petits, tout éperdus, le long des rangs,
ne peuvent même plus retrouver leurs mamans.

— Un surtout... qui me ressemble de plus en plus!
un surtout, que je vois — un surtout... a perdu

au grand vent poussiéreux, au grand soleil de joie,
son beau chapeau tout neuf, blanc de paille et de soie,
et je le vois... sur la route... qui court après
— et perd le défilé des «Messieurs» et des «Dames» —
court après — et fait rire de lui — court après,
aveuglé de soleil, de poussière et de larmes...

SUR CE GRAND CHEMIN GRIS...

«Je suis plus près de toi dans l'obscurité»
(*Pelléas et Mélisande*, acte IV, scène 3)

Sur ce Grand Chemin gris
où nous ont amenés deux sentiers de traverse,
nous voilà pris tous deux par l'orage et l'averse
et la nuit. Pas d'abris
en vue. Il va falloir marcher par les ornières
en guettant aux détours les premières lumières
lointaines d'un pays...
Il va falloir marcher en se donnant la main
— Voyageurs des mois gris, perdus aux grands chemins
devant soi, par la nuit...

*

Nous ne pourrons pas lire aux bornes des chemins,
nous ne pourrons pas lire à cause de la nuit,
de la nuit sans étoile, à cause de la pluie.

*

Et pourtant nous irons, aveugles et confiants
et contents de la route et contents de la vie,
comme si nous étions deux tout petits enfants
sur le chemin du bourg, sous un grand parapluie.

*

Nous irons au hasard, tous deux: une ombre, un pas...
Et nous pardonnerons à la nuit, dans les bois,
à la nuit sur nos pas, à la nuit qui fait perdre.
Puisque j'ai dit: «Viens près de moi,.. plus près de moi»,
de crainte de te perdre.
Puisque tu as, ce soir, osé prendre mes doigts,

65

dans l'ombre qui fait peur, avec tes doigts timides
pour ne plus avoir peur et pour que je te guide.

*

Nous sortirons parfois du chemin, tous les deux
et nous aurons parfois de l'eau jusqu'aux chevilles;
les rafales de vent, de pluie et de ramilles
arrêteront nos pas, et fermeront nos yeux…
Et nous n'en voudrons pas davantage à la pluie

Puisqu'elle est, quelque part, la seule pauvre amie
de ceux qui pensent, éveillés, jusqu'au matin,
et, tout seuls, dans leur lit, avec la fièvre aux mains,
l'écoutent, consolés, leur tenir compagnie
de son petit sanglot par la plaine endormie…
et ruisseler toute la nuit dans les jardins…

*

… Nous irons si longtemps, si longtemps, par la plaine
qu'à la fin… à la fin, exténuée, hors d'haleine
et le cœur gros, tu ne pourras plus faire un pas.
— Alors, c'est moi, soudain, qui porterai ta peine,
ta peine reposée et bercée à mon pas,
qui sera presque du bonheur, puisqu'il faudra
que je te prenne dans mes bras…

— Alors… Alors, il faudra bien que ces lointaines
ces premières lueurs lointaines d'un pays,
à mes yeux fatigués d'avoir fouillé la nuit,
finissent par briller, paisibles et soudaines.
… Rassurantes lueurs du bourg et des domaines
… lampes de la veillée et veilleuses lointaines
et foyer, quelque part, d'une auberge — lueur
de l'auberge où, ce soir, j'emporte ma compagne,

66

de l'auberge, là-bas, que tout ce soir je gagne,
ton cœur contre mon cœur...

Et dans la toile rude à l'odeur de campagne
où nous reposerons nos membres douloureux
en rêvant au bonheur tranquille des campagnes,
en parlant de la nuit et des chemins peureux,
— ta chair sera si douce et tiède et parfumée,
ta douce chair d'amour, ta chair de bien-aimée,
ta chair où l'on s'endort, ta chair consolatrice,
qu'elle sera pareille aux linges des églises,
délicats et divins, linges de soie et d'or,
que l'on met soigneusement autour des calices,
pour que le sang de ceux «tristes jusqu'à la mort»,
qui font l'étape, un soir, seuls avec une croix,
en laissant sur la route, où, silencieux, ils passent,
un peu de pauvre sang que des femmes ramassent,
— pour que ce sang précieux, dans les calices froids,
coulé des pieds, les soirs, coulé des faces lasses
— pour que ce sang des Christs ait moins mal et moins froid.

RONDE

«Nous n'irons plus au bois
Les lauriers sont coupés...»

Le soir est doux, la ronde est folle,
Donnez vos mains, ô mes frivoles,
Allons danser sous les tilleuls!...

Nos cœurs et vos jupes s'envolent;
le soir est bleu, mon âme est folle;
Allons tourner sous les tilleuls!...

*

... On tournera jusqu'au froid
avec «la belle que voilà»...

*

La fillette entre dans la ronde;
La place est brune, la ronde est blonde
Et le soir chante au pas des portes...

Mon âme est la fillette blonde:
Nous n'irons pas courir le monde!
Restons danser au pas des portes!...

*

... On a dansé jusqu'au froid
avec «la belle que voilà»...

*

Encore un tour avant la nuit!
Un tour, avant d'avoir grandi!
Un tour, et nous irons dormir...

Au dernier, sous les marronniers,
Au dernier tour, on a tourné..
on a tourné jusqu'à mourir!

*

… On a tourné jusqu'à mourir…

À TRAVERS LES ÉTÉS...

(À une Jeune Fille.
À une Maison.
À Francis Jammes.)

Attendue
à travers les étés qui s'ennuient dans les cours
en silence
et qui pleurent d'ennui..
Sous le soleil ancien de mes après-midi
lourds de silence,
solitaires et rêveurs d'amour
d'amours sous des glycines, à l'ombre, dans la cour
de quelque maison calme et perdue sous les branches,
À travers mes lointains, mes enfantins étés,
ceux qui rêvaient d'amour
et qui pleuraient d'enfance,

Vous êtes venue,
une après-midi chaude dans les avenues,
sous une ombrelle blanche,
avec un air étonné, sérieux,
un peu
penché comme mon enfance,
Vous êtes venue sous une ombrelle blanche.

Avec toute la surprise
inespérée d'être venue et d'être blonde,
de vous être soudain
mise
sur mon chemin,
et soudain d'apporter la fraîcheur de vos mains
avec, dans vos cheveux, tous les étés du monde.

*

Vous êtes venue..
Tout mon rêve au soleil
n'aurait jamais osé vous espérer si belle..
et pourtant, tout de suite, je vous ai reconnue.

Tout de suite, près de vous, fière et très demoiselle,
et une vieille dame gaie à votre bras,
il m'a semblé que vous me conduisiez, à pas
lents, − un peu, n'est-ce pas, un peu sous votre ombrelle −,
à la maison d'été, à mon rêve d'enfant..

.. à quelque maison calme avec des nids aux toits
et l'ombre des glycines, dans la cour, sur le pas
de la porte.. quelque maison à deux tourelles
avec, peut-être, un nom comme les livres de prix
qu'on lisait en juillet, quand on était petit..

Dites, vous m'emmeniez passer l'après-midi
Oh! qui sait où!... à «La Maison des Tourterelles».

*

Vous arriviez, là-bas,
dans tout le piaillement des moineaux sur le toit,
dans l'ombre de la grille qui se ferme.. Cela
fait s'effeuiller, du mur et des rosiers grimpants,
les pétales légers, embaumés et brûlants,
couleur de neige et couleur d'or, couleur de feu,
sur les fleurs des parterres et sur le vert des bancs,
et dans l'allée comme un chemin de Fête-Dieu.

Je vais entrer.. Nous allons suivre, tous les deux,
avec la vieille dame, l'allée où doucement
votre robe, ce soir, en la reconduisant,
balaiera des parfums couleur de vos cheveux.

Puis recevoir, tous deux,
dans l'ombre du salon,
des visites, où nous dirons
de jolis riens cérémonieux.

Ou bien lire avec vous auprès du pigeonnier
sur un banc de jardin, et toute la soirée,
aux roucoulements longs des colombes peureuses
et cachées, qui s'effarent de la page tournée,
lire avec vous, à l'ombre, sous le marronnier,
un roman d'autrefois, ou «Clara d'Ellébeuse».

Et rester là jusqu'au dîner jusqu'à la nuit,
à l'heure où l'on entend tirer de l'eau au puits
et jouer les enfants rieurs dans les sentes fraîchies..

*

C'est Là – qu'auprès de vous, ô ma lointaine,
je m'en allais..
et vous n'alliez,
avec mon rêve, sur vos pas,
qu'à mon rêve, Là-Bas,
à ce château dont vous étiez, douce et hautaine,
la châtelaine..

C'est Là – que nous allions – tous les deux, n'est-ce pas,
ce dimanche, à Paris, dans l'avenue lointaine
qui s'était faite alors, pour plaire à notre rêve,
plus silencieuse, et plus lointaine, et solitaire...
Puis, sur les quais déserts des berges de la Seine...
et puis après, plus près de vous, sur le bateau,
qui faisait un bruit calme de machine et d'eau...

CHANT DE ROUTE

«... des grandes routes où nul ne passe»
J. Laforgue.

Un conquérant, puis tous, chantent:

Nous avons eu la fièvre
de tes marais.
Nous avons eu la fièvre et nous sommes partis.

Nous étions avertis
qu'on ne trouvait
que du soleil
au plus profond de tes forêts.

Nous avons eu des histoires
de brancards
cassés,
de fers perdus,
de chevaux blessés,
d'ânes fourbus
et suants qui refusaient d'avancer.

Nous avons perdu la mémoire de ces histoires
que l'on raconte à l'arrivée;
nous n'avions pas l'espoir
d'arriver.

Nous avons pris les harnais
pour nous en faire
des souliers.
Nous sommes repartis, à pied dans tes genêts
qui font saigner les pieds
et nos pieds ont saigné,

et nos pieds ont séché
dans ta poussière,
en marchant,
et nous avons guéri leurs plaies
en écrasant,
en marchant,
le baume et les parfums sauvages de tes bruyères.

Nous aurions pu asseoir
au revers des fossés
nos corps fumants et harassés.
Nous n'avions rien à dire: nous n'avions pas d'espoirs.
Nous n'avions rien à dire; nous n'avions rien à boire.
Nous avons préféré la déroute
sans fin
des horizons et des routes,
des horizons défaits qui se refont plus loin
et des kilomètres qu'on laisse en arrière
dans la poussière
pour attraper ceux qu'on voit plus loin,
avec leur bornes
indicatrices de villes aux noms lointains
aux noms qui sonnent
comme les cailloux de tes chemins
sous nos talons.

Nous n'atteindrons jamais les villes de merveilles
qui ne sont que des noms
qui sonnent,
les noms des villes qui sont mortes au soleil.

Mais nous, nous voulons vivre au Soleil
de tes cieux
avec nos crânes en feu,
et faire sonner sans fin les étapes de gloire

avec nos pieds d'étincelles.
Nous avons pour chanter des gosiers de victoire
et nous avons nos chants pour nous verser à boire
et nous avons la fièvre
de tes marais séchés au grand soleil
de tes routes de poussière
de tes villes de mirage.

Nous avons eu la fièvre
de tes forêts sans ombre – et tes bruyères des sables
avec leurs regards roux et leurs parfums sauvages
nous ont donné la fièvre.

SOUS CE TIÈDE RESTANT…

2 septembre

Sous ce tiède restant
de soleil,
par ce beau temps
doux de septembre
parfumé, clair et doré comme une abeille,
je songe à celle
qu'était, dans le verger, à petits pas pressés,
dix ans passées,
la petite vieille.

Et je voudrais, comme l'autre année,
entrer là-bas secouer les poires,
dans son verger abandonné,
et la croire,
son mouchoir noué autour des tempes,
son visage
ridé tendu, tout à sa tâche de Septembre,
là, sous les poiriers,
à emplir son tablier,
ou à étendre
de toute sa vieille petite âme villageoise
des linges frais lavés sur les haies de framboises.

Je sais qu'elle est, par ces derniers beaux temps,
une âme, là-bas, dans les jardins,
à mi-chemin
de la côte et qu'elle m'attend.
Puisqu'il y a toujours des histoires à dire
sur des bancs
des histoires anciennes de son jeune temps,
sous le vieux ciel doux de Septembre,

et des poires à cueillir
dans les jardins de ses enfants
des poires qui sentent comme son armoire, il y a dix ans,
le miel et l'ambre.

Peut-être que là-bas
personne ne sent
que tout cela c'est son âme qui bat
doucement.
Il n'y a que moi.
Personne ne saurait
ouvrir la barrière,
entrer,
sans troubler la prière
de l'enclos silencieux et du verger désert
où son âme se plaît.

Personne au village
ne sait, personne.
Et c'est moi, tous les ans, qui fais ce pèlerinage
avant que le grand vent fou d'automne
de ses grandes mains brutales et folles
secoue, en hurlant, les vergers,
casse les branches et fasse sauter
les poires oubliées
et souffle – comme un soir, il y a dix années,
et comme chaque année,
après mon départ,
souffle, en hurlant, la chandelle
et l'âme de la petite vieille,
un soir,
par les vallons et par le ciel.

PREMIÈRES BRUMES DE SEPTEMBRE...

«Crois-moi, c'est bien fini jusqu'à l'année prochaine.»
J. Laforgue.

Premières brumes de septembre
sur les fougères, les bruyères, dans les landes,
par les chasses, dans les sapins.

Premiers feux dans les bourgs, flambées de grand matin
qui craquent et luisent dans les salles
obscures des auberges, des fermes et des chaumières
matinales.

Venu de loin par les frais grands chemins
dans sa voiture couverte,
l'épicier ambulant s'arrête
pour causer, vendre et se chauffer les mains,
et laisse son attelage qui grelotte
et fume aux portes
entr'ouvertes.

Et j'aperçois aux murs, par éclats de lumière,
avant qu'on ait ouvert
les volets,
les images et les chromos qu'on verra tout l'hiver
rougeâtrement illuminés,
représenter au-dessus de la cheminée,
dans les salles obscures
et basses des chaumières, des fermes et des auberges,
de belles dames avec des manchons et des fourrures
dans des paysages de neige.

Et j'entends: «Pas chaud, ce matin! – Voilà les froids.
– Il a dû geler blanc, cette nuit, dans les bois.»

– Oh! nous étions si bien partis pour les étés!
va-t-il falloir
ce soir
fermer encore toutes les portes des châteaux
et s'en retourner?
s'en revenir, enveloppés dans les manteaux,
le long des routes en châtaignes
dégringolées,
gelés,
dans les voitures à ânes et les calèches toutes pleines
de consternés et petits désespoirs,
avec les vacances finies qui s'en reviennent.

ET MAINTENANT QUE C'EST LA PLUIE...

Et maintenant que c'est la pluie et le grand vent
de Janvier
et que les vitres de la serre
où je me suis réfugié
font, sous la pluie, leur petit bruit de verre
toute la journée,
et que le vent, qui rabat la fumée des cheminées,
dégrafe et soulève
les vignes vierges de la tonnelle,
Je ne sais plus où Elle est... Où est-elle?

*

À pas pleins d'eau, par les allées,
dans le sable mouillé
du jardin
qui nous fut à tous deux notre rêve de Juin,
Elle s'en est allée...

et la Maison
où nous avions, tout cet été,
sous les feuilles des avenues qu'on arrosait,
imaginé
de passer notre vie comme une belle saison,

la Maison,
dans mon cœur, abandonnée, est froide
avec son toit
d'ardoise luisant d'eau,
et ses nids de moineaux
dénichés et pourris qui penchent aux corniches
et traînent dans le vent...

*

Il va bientôt faire nuit,
et le grand vent bruineux tourne les parapluies
et mouille au visage
les dames qui reviennent du village
et ouvrent la grille…

Mon amie
Ô Demoiselle
qui n'êtes pas ici,
cette heure-ci
passe, et la grille ne grince pas,
je ne vous attends pas,
je ne soulève
pas le rideau
pour vous voir, dans le vent et l'eau,
venir.

Cette heure passe, mon amie,
Ce n'est pas une heure de notre vie…
et nous l'aurions aimée, pourtant, comme toutes celles
de toute la vie
apportée simplement dans vos mains graves de dame belle.

*

Vous êtes partie…

Il bruine
dans les allées
qui ont mouillé
vos chevilles fines.

Il bruine dans les marronniers
confus et sombres
et sur les bancs où, cet été, à l'ombre,

avec l'été
vous vous seriez assise, blonde!

Il bruine sur la maison et sur la grille et dans les ifs
de l'entrée
que, pour la dernière fois
peut-être je regarde, en songeant à mi-voix
peut-être pour la dernière fois:
«Elle est très loin... où est-elle... son front pensif
appuyé à quelle croisée?»

*

À la tombée de la nuit,
je vais fermer, aux fenêtres d'ici,
les volets qui battent et se mouillent,
et j'irai sur la pelouse
rentrer
un jeu de croquet oublié qui se rouille.

DANS LE CHEMIN QUI S'ENFONCE…

Dans le chemin qui s'enfonce à la ferme
au soleil taché d'ombre, entre deux haies
d'où sortent, pour rentrer, des poulets –
Apparue
à la barrière d'un champ,
venue à travers blés,
tenant d'un geste négligent
la robe fraîche et l'ombrelle qui traînent –
Vous voici revenue,
par le chemin de noisetiers,
vers la maison de notre amour abandonné.

Ô cérémonieuse amie lointaine, vous ne trouverez plus
la Maison-Belle de l'été passé:
l'autre été, l'autre amour
sont passés – et revenus
au soleil dur, parmi les paysans grossiers,
vers les pauvres maisons d'autrefois et de toujours,

Et pourtant,
ô ma sérieuse amie, ma silencieuse, ma fidèle
lointaine amie, n'ayez pas peur pour venir, pour me suivre
chez les paysans graves, silencieux et lents,
dans la cour où l'on attelle
la jument,
pour vous asseoir sur la planche de cuir
brûlante qui balance,
attachée par deux cordes derrière le siège
de la voiture.

Ouvrez votre ombrelle
comme ça...
là.

Le paysan va vous dire: Mademoiselle
vous auriez été mieux sur le devant.
Dites-lui doucement
comme si vous existiez, que non.

Et restons,
balancés, secoués, à regarder...

On s'arrête... ho...
— là! sur la route devenue,
après des côtes et des descentes et des tournants dans le petit pays,
    la rue
où le charron
a mis sécher une voiture;
où, du côté de l'ombre,
les femmes cousent au bord des fenêtres obscures:
on s'arrête en plein soleil,
devant une maison.

N'ayez pas peur pour passer sur le pont
du fossé;
J'enlève le loquet
de la barrière blanche; et, sous la treille,
dans la petite cour aux murs de bouquets,
enfin, malhabilement, enfin!
voici vos mains
sur la poignée noire de la porte dure.

On ne nous attend pas.
Personne n'est sorti, la main sur les yeux,
pour nous voir arriver. La voiture s'en va.

Nous sommes là, tous deux, n'osant pas
ouvrir, ou pousser le volet qui coupe en deux
la porte paysanne, et apparaître aux vieux.

N'ayez pas peur… que de ne pas assez
follement
aimer la folle impossible journée…

Et repartons… Allons-nous-en
vers les toits
semés entre les arbres, sous le ciel fleuri blanc,
éblouissants, à l'horizon
— comme des morceaux de cailloux ou de miroirs,
dans l'herbe et les fleurs de blé noir.

Ô Taille-Mince,
on va dire, dans les champs,
que votre taille tiendrait dans
la ceinture des deux mains ainsi jointes.

Ô Blonde,
Ô ardente apparue, ô cheveux blonds,
on va vouloir vous couronner,
pour vous faire honneur, de la fleur
des moissons —
et de soleil, cueillis au faîte des batteuses
qu'on entend lointainement ronfler par la campagne
et haleter, et qui crachent,
dans les cours, la paille poussiéreuse.

Oh! mon amie,
j'appuierai ma tête
j'appuierai ma tête sur votre robe
dans la salle basse et froide où nous sommes assis,
et ce sera comme si

depuis l'aube
nous étions partis à travers blés pour la folle journée;
comme si, tous les deux, nous avions entendu,
en passant au bourg,
le roulement lourd
de la porte humble et du volet vermoulu,
et, en passant à travers champs,
le haletant bourdonnement des machines des champs;
puis ce sera comme si nous étions arrivés
au soir, dans la salle basse de la ferme inconnue
où nous irons demander du lait.

SOME NOTES ON THE TRANSLATION

JULIAN BARNES came to Alain-Fournier late – he was in his late thirties when he first read *Le Grand Meaulnes*,[1] and for me it was later still, for I first read Fournier's novel in my late forties (in 2013). I was living in Brittany with Anita Marsh, who was recuperating from one bout of chemotherapy undertaken in London and about to start another in St Brieuc. We settled down to watch our favourite French television programme, *Le Grand Librairie*, presented by François Busnel. The book-review edition focused on French writers who had died during the First World War. Alain-Fournier's *Le Grand Meaulnes* was mentioned, and its massive impact on the French literary imagination. One academic mentioned the poems of Alain-Fournier in *Miracles*, which we subsequently discovered had never been translated into English.

The anticipation and excitement on receiving a 1957 Oxford World Classics edition of *The Lost Domain: Le Grand Meaulnes* and a 1924 Gallimard edition of *Miracles* is still palpable. The hardback pocket edition of *The Lost Domain*, translated by Frank Davison and introduced by Alan Pryce-Jones, with its front cover of broken gates and tilting pillars behind which a gravel path flanked by fruit trees leads to an abandoned château or manor house, is still my favourite rendering of Fournier's classic. I read Fournier's novel and Yves Bonnefoy's *L'Arrière-pays* in the café at L'hôpital Yves le Foll in St Brieuc, during breaks from the treatment rooms six floors above.

Perhaps I, too, was transported, Peter Pan-like, by Fournier's magical tale, a journey, but also a grail-like quest, with Meaulnes

---

1. Julian Barnes, *The Guardian*, Friday 13 April 2012. A Francophile, Barnes rediscovered his love for Alain-Fournier in 2011–12 and took part in a BBC Radio 3 programme that sought to explore the terrain around Fournier's childhood home. Barnes feels that Fournier's oeuvre is indicative of 'a last explosion of Romanticism' before the onset of World War 1.

searching for something, while unable to articulate convincingly the nature of the thing he searches for. My search, or dream-like hope, in these writing and reading sessions at the café was for a miracle: that Anita would be cured, and would live, and that we could exist eternally in a lost Eden.[2]

I was aware that my personal feelings toward Anita sometimes bordered, Fournier-like, on the idealistic, if not the obsessive. There was something of a prophecy come true about our liaison, given that I had dreamed about being her lover ten years earlier when we were work colleagues in a London bookshop (while I was still happily married to another woman). It was ten years later that we came together, a year after my divorce. By this time, Anita was already receiving treatment for secondary cancer at Charing Cross Hospital in London.

Our love had been given a sentence of tangible finitude. However, I was in denial about its termination, planning even in the last few months of her life for a French idyll in southern Brittany where Nantes nods in the direction of the Loire, heading toward that landscape of Bonnefoy's Tours and Fournier's Sologne. I identified, then, with Meaulnes' obsessive pursuit of the beautiful and mysterious Yvonne de Galais in *Le Grand Meaulnes,* empathised with the narrator's unrequited love and sense of loss in the poems in *Miracles.*

I felt I could almost breathe the air with Fournier on Ascension Day in 1905, could see in Renoir's portraits of women reading or walking in gardens, shaded by their parasols, the same mysterious vision – both Fournier's real obsession, Yvonne de Quiévrecourt, and Anita herself.

John Fowles, invoking the work of Georges Bataille in *Eroticism and Death,* suggests that Fournier's writing demonstrates that 'paradox at the heart of the human condition, that the satisfaction

---

2. Allan Massie thinks *Le Grand Meaulnes* is a search for a lost Eden, *Daily Telegraph,* 12 October 2013.
3. John Fowles, 'Afterword', *The Wanderer,* Signet, 1971.

of the desire is also the death of the desire';[3] the implication that what kept Fournier's love for Yvonne de Quiévrecourt so potently alive was a state of fervour concerning a love that was to be immaculately unconsummated. All the other women in Fournier's life that he had actual relationships with – another Yvonne (Yvonne G.), Jeanne Bruneau, Loulette, Simone – were poor imitations of a portrait of Yvonne de Quiévrecourt.

In my case, and countering this theory, satisfaction of desire with Anita Marsh led to more desire, the singular possession and ownership of my own favourite portrait contingent upon the vagaries of cancer, and leading me to a landscape of 'desert places'. By reading Fournier, I was both escaping, and in denial of, Anita's passing. In breaks from my own writing, and while she was hooked up to intravenous tubes, I was planning the food on the table for the evening meal over which I would ask her to be my co-translator of the poems in *Miracles*.

*   *   *

Three days after undergoing an operation at a London hospital in August 2013, during which a biopsy was taken to determine if I had cancer, I hobbled to the Poetry Place, 22 Betterton Street where Anouche Sherman had organised an evening dedicated to French poetry in translation. I duly read three versions of Alain-Fournier's poems that Anita Marsh and I had translated in the spring of 2013. Anthony Howell was in the audience and I met him, briefly, at the soirée after the reading. He expressed a long-standing admiration for *Le Grand Meaulnes* and was intrigued and encouraging of the 'lovely project' Anita and I had been working on, translating the eight long prose poems in the 1924 Gallimard edition of *Miracles*. He suggested two outlets for the Fournier poems: his own online Grey Suit poem stream and *The Fortnightly Review*, where he is a contributing editor. Some of the translations appeared there and soon after others were accepted by *Acumen* and *The French Literary Review*. Anita Marsh knew of these publishing achievements before she died on 17 October 2013.

In the summer of 2014, after many months of depression, I vowed to honour Anita's life and work by finding a publisher for our manuscript. I read and researched Fournier's life and works and wrote an introduction to the poems. I then contacted Anthony Howell and asked if he would read (and potentially edit) the manuscript. Fluent in French, he showed me certain discrepancies in my own versions, and so I decided to leave Anita's notebook with him, so that he could work on the poems in his own way. The meandering evolution of this translation from dreamy idea to publication would not have been possible without his input. He argued that we should 'have faith in the mundane', which I took to mean paying attention to the detail in the French original and (even more profoundly) that we should have faith in Alain-Fournier.

He subsequently found six more poems in a later edition than ours, and translated these too. I feel that this 'labour of love' is a genuine collaboration between us all.

ANTHONY COSTELLO

NOT SIMPLY THE MEANING

ANTHONY COSTELLO contacted me early in 2014. He sent me the versions he had done of the poems of Alain-Fournier. These intrigued me. I had loved reading *Le Grand Meaulnes* as a young man. Anita Marsh, already dying of cancer, had made word-for-word translations of the texts for him, a final act. I never met her. I wish I had. He visited, and left me the beautiful notebook with a cover decorated with a garden in spring in which Anita had written out the words in French; the lines numbered, and the words in English opposite, with their alternatives and ambiguities in brackets. He also left me the battered Gallimard edition, its pages turning brown, of *Miracles,* the collection of short prose works by Fournier which includes these eight visions, apparently forming his entire poetic oeuvre, and a comprehensive introduction by Jacques Rivière. While Anthony's versions were the prompts which got me started, I mainly worked from the French, and from Anita's notes.

On purchasing my own copies of *Miracles*, I discovered that the 2011 Livre de Poche edition included six poems that were not in the original Gallimard edition used by Anthony and Anita. These I have translated and have added in the order they appear in that 2011 publication.

It should be noted that while I have tried to be as true to the originals as I can be, my versions are not exactly literal translations, or, to put it another way, I seek to translate the poetry, not simply the meaning. Thus, 'Sur la nacelle...':

> Sur la nacelle
> Une ombrelle
> De satin.
>
> La tache est rouge
> L'eau ne bouge
> Ce matin.

This might be correctly translated as:

> On the skiff,
> A parasol
> Of satin.

> The stain is red,
> The water does not move
> This morning.

But the short lines are cross-connected by rhyme in the original, and it is this poetic music that I seek to capture, yes, even at the cost of tampering with the meaning: *Nacelle* and *parasol*, *satin* and *matin* . . . one senses that the poem grew out of these coincidences, and so I seek for equivalents in my own language. *Nacelle* being the French name for a type of boat, I keep it in my version, but I can't retain *matin* without sounding like Wallace Stevens, and so I find a rhyme for *satin* that works for me in English:

> On the nacelle,
> A parasol
> Of satin.

> A stain of red,
> A breeze to seize
> Your hat in.

Out of sheer enthusiasm, it is easy to go too far, and find oneself writing one's own poem. This I have held back on, very much helped by Luke Allan of Carcanet, and Peter Jay, who set this book. Their suggestions have been appreciated, as well as their willingness to put up with all the fine-tuning it has taken to get these poems into another language. I would also like to thank Gwendolyn Leick and Chloe Chard for resolving queries about the original French.

ANTHONY HOWELL